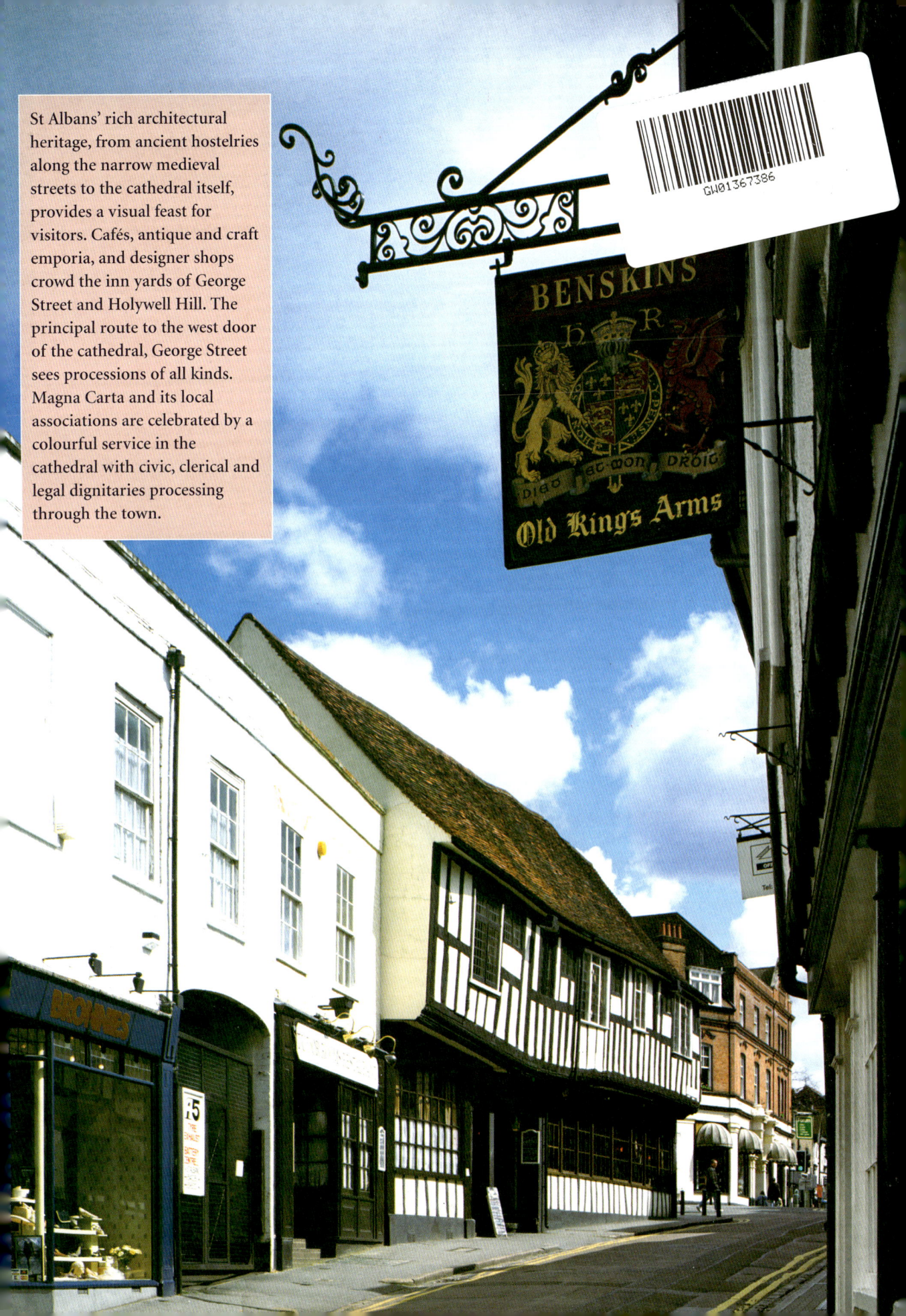

St Albans' rich architectural heritage, from ancient hostelries along the narrow medieval streets to the cathedral itself, provides a visual feast for visitors. Cafés, antique and craft emporia, and designer shops crowd the inn yards of George Street and Holywell Hill. The principal route to the west door of the cathedral, George Street sees processions of all kinds. Magna Carta and its local associations are celebrated by a colourful service in the cathedral with civic, clerical and legal dignitaries processing through the town.

The City of St Albans Tour Guides provide guided walks and talks around the town on Wednesdays and Saturdays, starting from the Clock Tower. These reflect the exciting and diverse history of the city:

'Historic St Albans' tells of the city from the time when Ulsinus, one of the early Saxon Abbots, first laid out the market. He also established the parish churches of St Michael, St Stephen and St Peter in 948.

'Wars of the Roses' charts the progress of the two battles of St Albans (1455 and 1461). Henry VI stayed at Hall Place in Bowgate during this period and many soldiers who fought in the battles are buried in St Peter's churchyard alongside.

The 'Pubs, chapels and stagecoaching days' walk reflects the sacred and profane in the city's history. St Albans was traditionally a dissenting community, and supported Cromwell's Parliamentarians. Independent chapels and meeting houses were established early on. John Wesley visited the city and Bunyan lodged nearby. Brewing has gone on since Roman times, providing over the years for residents, traders, pilgrims and stagecoach passengers alike. The city still has many excellent pubs and restaurants.

The municipal gardens behind St Peter's Street.

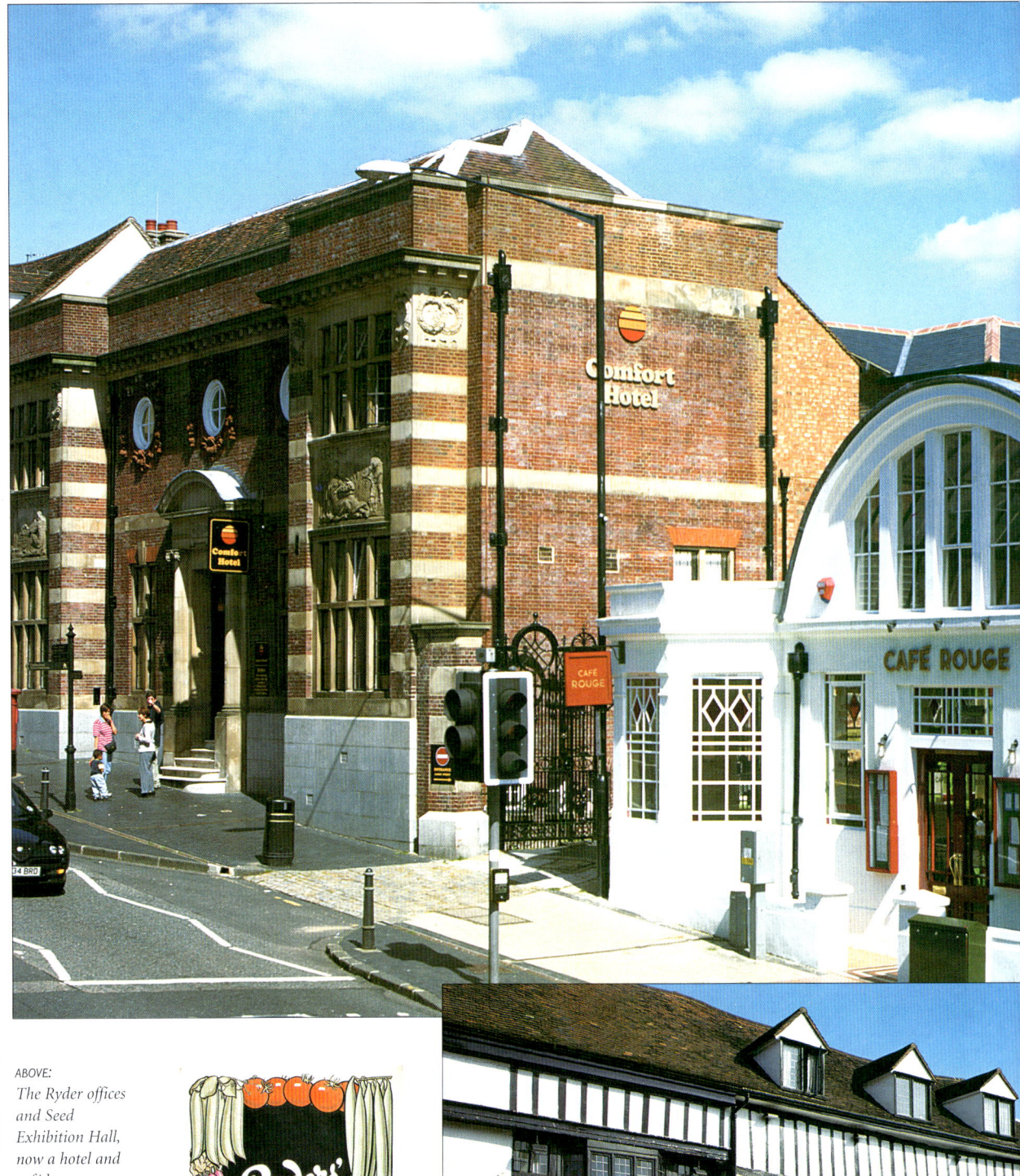

ABOVE:
The Ryder offices and Seed Exhibition Hall, now a hotel and café bar.

RIGHT:
Seeds for suburban gardeners.

CENTRE:
The White Hart Inn, Holywell Hill.

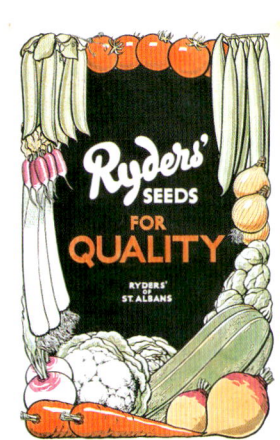

THE MARKET

The Saturday market, established in the 10th century, attracts a host of visitors from London and the neighbouring towns. Full of colour and surprises, it is overlooked by the striking façade of the classical town hall. In Market Place itself, visitors can climb the 93 steps of the city's Clock Tower for a spectacular view of the market, St Peter's Street and the cathedral (more correctly named 'the Cathedral and Abbey Church of St Alban').

Down amongst the traders, who now cry their wares on Wednesdays too, most things can be found on one or other of over a hundred stalls. Sovereign Alley, linking Market Place with Chequer Street, is a lasting reminder of the passageways around the market before permanent buildings overtook the shambles and stalls. Its name alludes to the exchange of coins during a by-election campaign of 1851, when supporters of the Spencers and the Grimstons paid off the freemen for the promise of their votes for one of the borough's two seats in Parliament. This bribery led to the people of St Albans losing their right to vote for over 30 years.

Chequer Street leads through the busy Peahen junction, then steeply down Holywell Hill. St Albans was on the original coaching route between London and Chester via Roman Watling Street, and it is said that an additional pair of horses was needed to pull up this stretch. Near where Sopwell Lane joins the hill, on the site of The Bull, once one of the largest inns in the country, is one of the city's best 20th-century buildings. Here were the offices of Samuel Ryder, entrepreneur, philanthropist and one time mayor of the borough. The site, with its 'Arts and Crafts' façade and the Seed Exhibition Hall next door, is today dedicated to the hospitality industry, restored and reopened as a hotel and café bar.

Ryder's success came from the small packets of seeds he cultivated for suburban gardeners, but it is the cup he gave to establish the famous transatlantic golfing competition for which he is internationally renowned.

LEFT:
St Albans market with the old town hall.

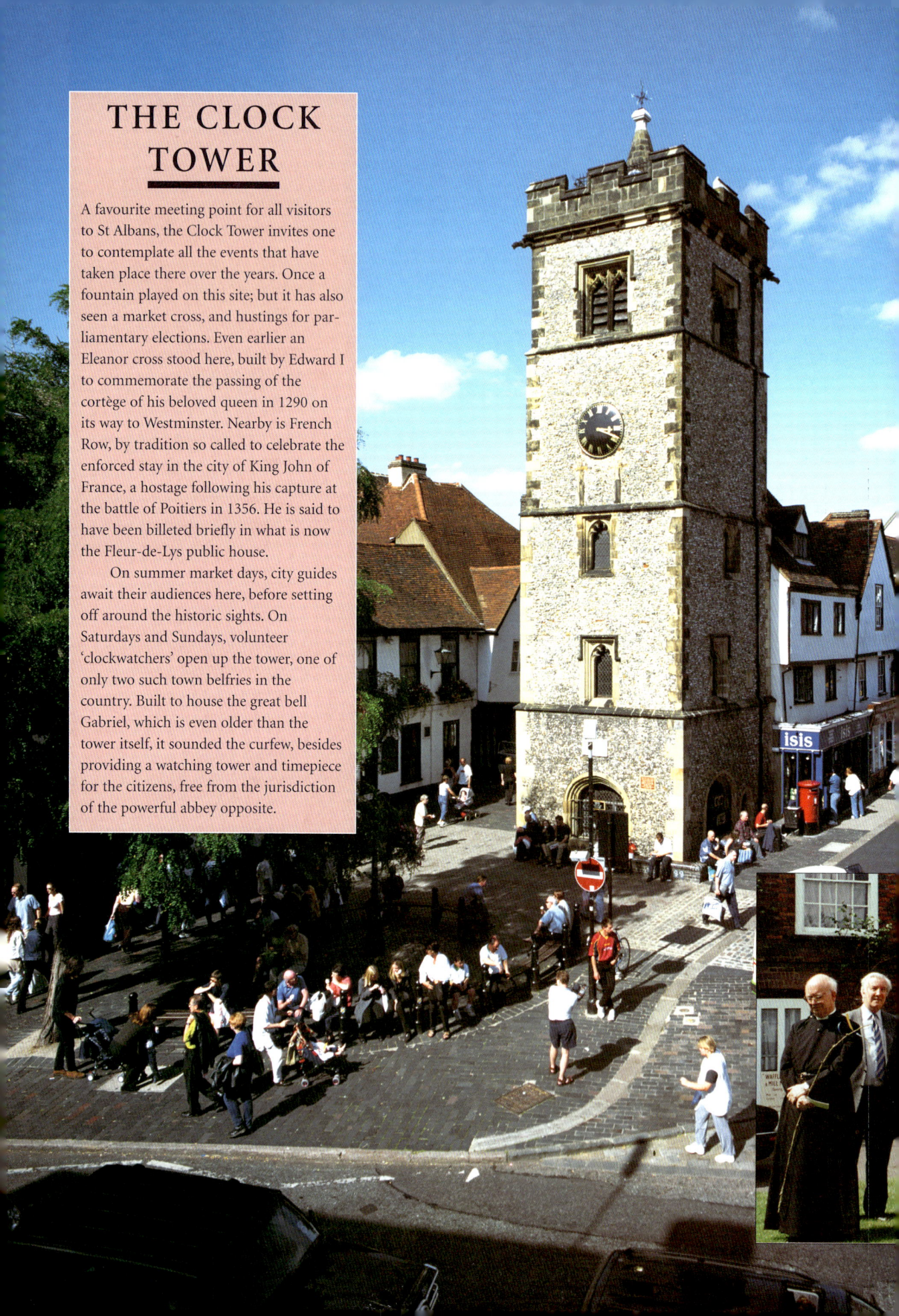

THE CLOCK TOWER

A favourite meeting point for all visitors to St Albans, the Clock Tower invites one to contemplate all the events that have taken place there over the years. Once a fountain played on this site; but it has also seen a market cross, and hustings for parliamentary elections. Even earlier an Eleanor cross stood here, built by Edward I to commemorate the passing of the cortège of his beloved queen in 1290 on its way to Westminster. Nearby is French Row, by tradition so called to celebrate the enforced stay in the city of King John of France, a hostage following his capture at the battle of Poitiers in 1356. He is said to have been billeted briefly in what is now the Fleur-de-Lys public house.

On summer market days, city guides await their audiences here, before setting off around the historic sights. On Saturdays and Sundays, volunteer 'clockwatchers' open up the tower, one of only two such town belfries in the country. Built to house the great bell Gabriel, which is even older than the tower itself, it sounded the curfew, besides providing a watching tower and timepiece for the citizens, free from the jurisdiction of the powerful abbey opposite.

St Albans

St Albans is now a cathedral city of some 75,000 inhabitants, but until the late 19th century the borough, as bounded by the medieval Tonman ditch, registered fewer than 4,000 souls. The line of the 4-mile (7km) ditch defined the land granted by a charter of Edward VI in 1553 to form the borough. It incorporated the abbey parish, and the urban parts of the parishes of St Peter, St Stephen and St Michael around it. A centuries-old ceremony, still continued today, affirms the ancient boundary. On Rogation Sunday in May each year the Mayor, city guides and worthy citizens walk round beating the bounds with willow wands, confirming the area of the Mayor's jurisdiction.

Tucked away behind a splendid brick wall, directly opposite the church of St Peter, can be found the prettiest council houses in the district, the Pemberton almshouses, now taken over from the original charity. Prompted by remorse at having accidentally shot a poor widow, Roger Pemberton endowed this row of six cottages in his will. They were built in 1627 and have housed elderly widows ever since.

MAIN:
The Clock Tower on market day.

LEFT:
Beating the bounds on Rogation Sunday.

ABOVE:
The Pemberton almshouses.

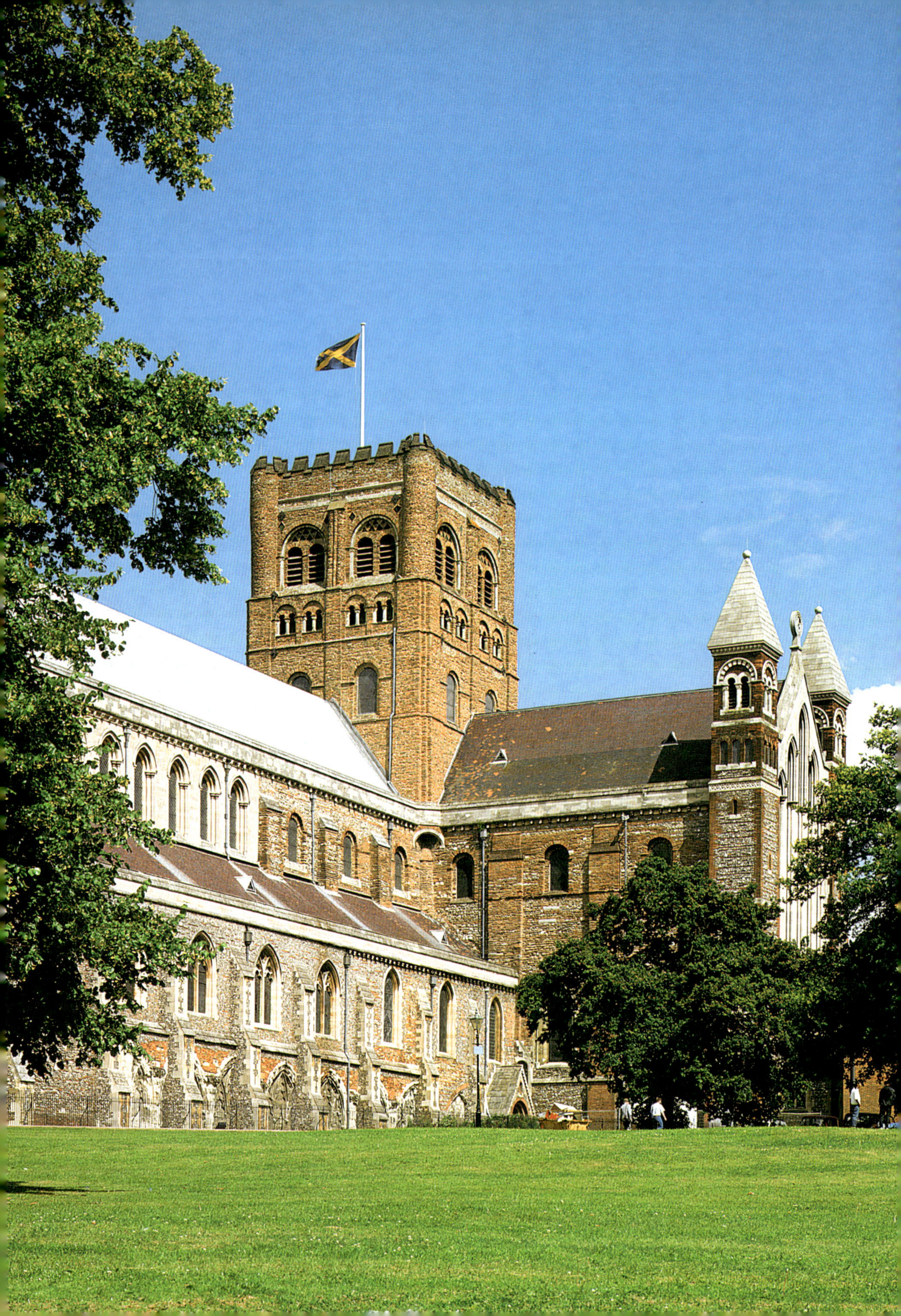

THE CATHEDRAL

The abbey church of St Alban had been a site of pilgrimage even before the 8th century when Offa, King of Mercia, commanded Willegod to found a Benedictine monastery here in honour of Alban, the first British Christian martyr. The saint's origins and the detail surrounding his fate are uncertain. Whether the 'hill with flowers', on which tradition says he died, is the abbey site, we may never be sure. It is fact, however, that Alban was a citizen of the earlier Roman city of Ve:ulamium at the foot of the hill, and that a shrine to his martyrdom has been consistently visited as a holy place for more than 12 centuries.

The vast history of the church is mirrored by its splendid and diverse architecture. The creation of a new diocese of St Albans in 1877 was opportune for this fascinating building. In 1539 the abbey had been dissolved by order of King Henry VIII and all of its buildings but the church and the gate house destroyed. It was bought 14 years later by the townspeople as their parish church, but maintenance costs proved prohibitive and the building fell into disrepair. Despite structural reinforcement by Sir George Gilbert Scott, more work was needed. A local benefactor, Lord Grimthorpe, offered to pay for a complete refurbishment, but controversially insisted on the replacement of several sections in the neo-Gothic style fashionable at the time. This now dominates the already diverse range of styles represented.

Massive Norman piers in the quire, transepts and nave remain from the time of Paul de Caen's rebuilding in 1077 and on them wall paintings from the 13th and 14th centuries can still be seen.

The shrine of St Alban, overseen by a handsome 15th-century watching loft, is a focus for today's visitors just as it was for medieval pilgrims. Duke Humphrey of Gloucester's tomb is also of particular note. After the 1553 purchase, the 13th-century Lady Chapel at the east end was converted into a grammar school and for many years remained sealed off from the rest of the building.

Supported and loved by the whole community, the cathedral today is always busy. In addition to holding regular services, it plays host to local people of many other faiths. Concerts, exhibitions and, every two years, the St Albans International Organ Festival keep the building constantly alive.

To match this spiritual activity, the cathedral's physical appearance is continuously being enhanced. In 1989 the Rose Window was reglazed, with modern stained glass lights donated by local company Laporte. It was unveiled by the late Diana, Princess of Wales, thus continuing her family's links with St Albans. Her ancestor Sarah Jennings of Water End married John Churchill, later 1st Duke of Marlborough. The couple regarded the town as their principal residence, despite the splendours of Blenheim, the palace given to them by a grateful nation for the Duke's successful campaigns in European wars.

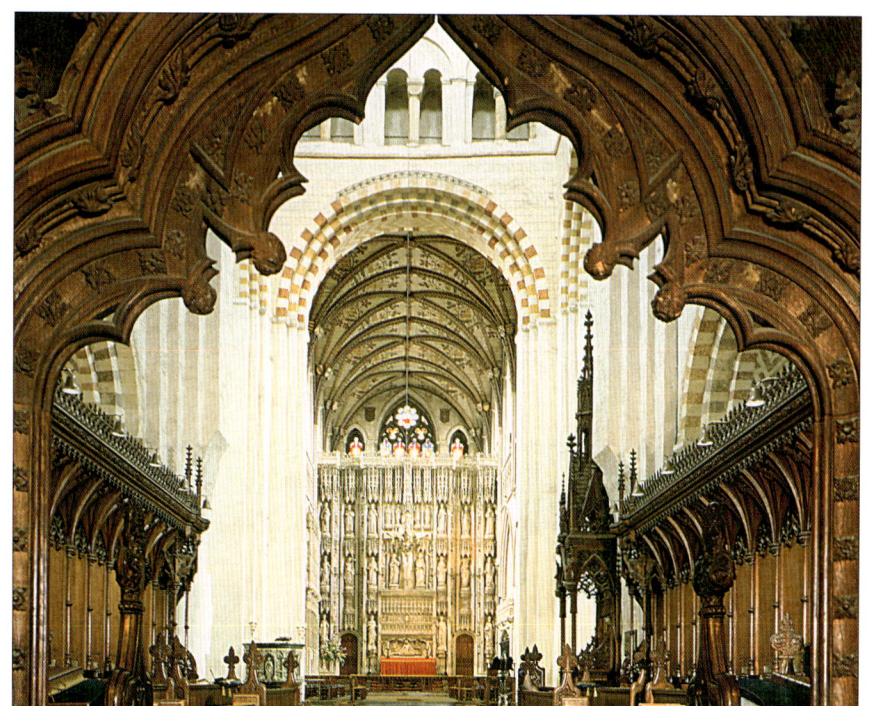

ABOVE RIGHT: The crossing and tower ceiling.

LEFT: St Albans Cathedral from the south-west.

BELOW: The view through the quire screen to the high altar.

ST ALBANS

VERULAMIUM PARK

The old abbey gateway, with the abbey church itself, is all that remains of the monastery, once one of the wealthiest and most important in the country. From there a lane leads down to the magnificent Verulamium Park. Here, the river Ver forms the boundary of the old monastery grounds. Close by, next to the old silk mills, is The Fighting Cocks, said to be the oldest inhabited public house in England. One can imagine the fights that took place in the old cockpit, or the sight of Oliver Cromwell and his Roundhead soldiers relaxing here as they passed through St Albans in the course of their Civil War campaigns.

From the park's beautiful lake, the cathedral dominates the horizon. The recycled Roman bricks of its stocky tower – the original short spire was removed in the 19th century – clearly show its architectural links with Roman Verulamium. During the Easter youth pilgrimage each year, thousands of youngsters make the journey from their home parish churches to congregate in the Abbey Orchard.

BELOW:
The Cathedral and Abbey Church of St Alban seen from Verulamium Park.

RIGHT:
The old abbey gate house, now part of St Albans School.

ROMAN ST ALBANS

Verulamium was one of the three greatest Roman cities in Britain. Established at a convenient point one day's journey from Londinium (London) on the principal route to the North, it superseded an existing Celtic settlement, Verlamion, named after its location on marshy ground near the river. The city flourished from around AD50 to at least AD429, although all the legions had been recalled to Rome by 409. For 300 years, during the *pax Romana* (Roman peace), few disturbances took place, and it is believed there was much intermarriage with local people. The city had the title *municipium* with the effect that all free inhabitants, whether Roman or British, could call themselves citizens. Alban was a citizen, thought to have been a soldier, executed because of his refusal to renounce his Christian beliefs.

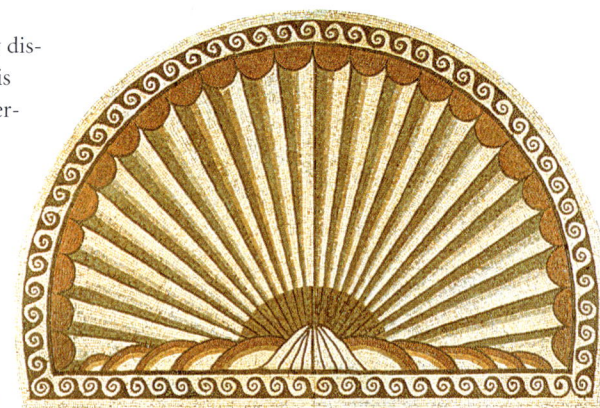

The earliest Roman settlement, made of timber, was sacked and burned by the famous warrior queen Boudicca on her march from Londinium in AD61. The city was gradually rebuilt and extended in stone and brick after this disaster, but, despite extensive archaeological excavations, little can be seen above ground today. Two sections of the city wall are visible in Verulamium Park, and protected inside a small building in the park is a Roman hypocaust (underfloor heating system) for a once splendid townhouse which also has a fine mosaic floor. The hypocaust is open at the same times as nearby Verulamium Museum.

The museum is to be found at the west end of the park, close to the site of Verulamium's great basilica. It was built to house Sir Mortimer Wheeler's finds of the 1930s, and is now entered through a magnificent rotunda in the Roman style. Some of the finest treasures of Roman Britain are here including some spectacular mosaics. One should allow at least an hour to visit it.

City guides conduct walks in the park and at the Roman theatre on Sundays in summer, and give talks on Roman topics in the museum on Saturday afternoons throughout the year.

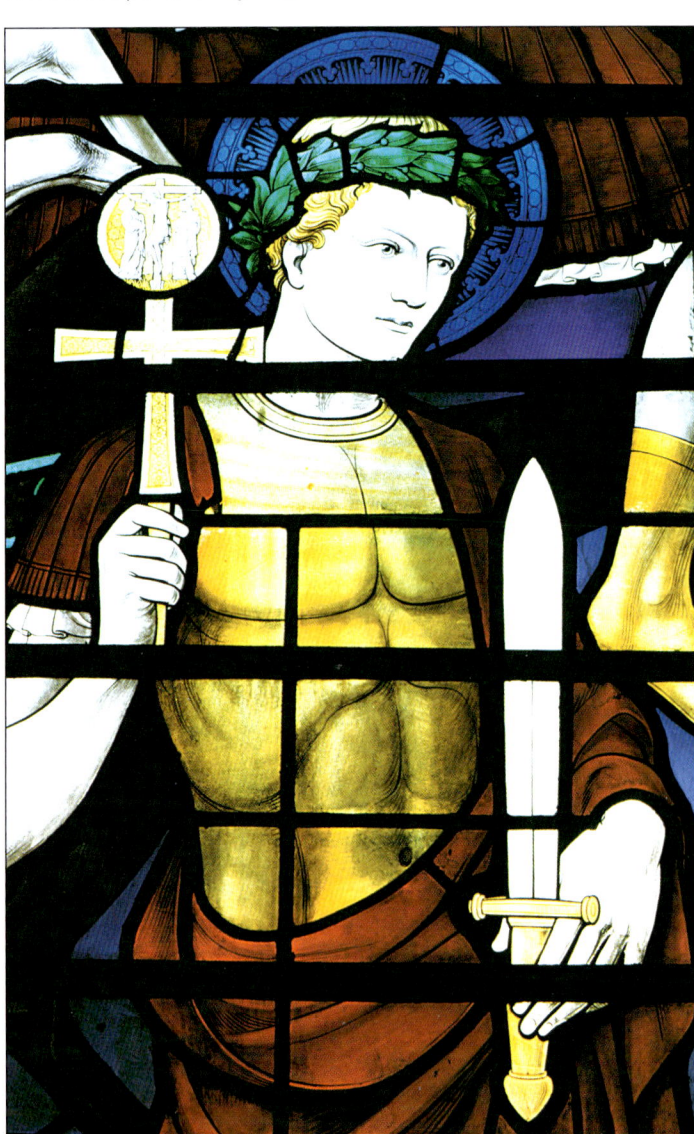

ABOVE: *Alban, with his unique cross, depicted in the cathedral.*

LEFT:
A shell mosaic exhibited in Verulamium Museum.

RIGHT:
The rotunda entrance to Verulamium Museum.

BELOW:
Part of the Verulamium city wall at the causeway entrance to the park.

ST ALBANS

GORHAMBURY AND THE ROMAN THEATRE

Although much of the Roman history of St Albans still remains to be discovered, excavations on the Verulamium site have revealed one of the few Roman theatres built in Britain. Its foundations and stage form some of the only visible remains of the stone and brick-built city. Originally constructed around AD140, it may have been extended eventually to accommodate up to 5,000 people. Situated on the private estate of the Earl of Verulam, it is even today used occasionally for theatrical productions. Behind the theatre, a temple of even larger proportions is known to have stood; and nearby are the remains of workshops and houses of Roman citizens where the beautiful little bronze Venus pictured below was found.

The path past the theatre leads into the estate of Gorhambury, another fine monument to the history of St Albans. The house which once stood on this site was built for Nicholas Bacon, the father of Francis Bacon, the celebrated philosopher, writer, politician and royal favourite. Gorhambury was known far and wide and was visited by Queen Elizabeth I.

Now ruined and an English Heritage site, the first house has been superseded by a Palladian mansion which is home to the Verulam family, although their descent has not been a direct line from the Bacons.

With a magnificent collection of portraits and some very fine furniture, the interior can be viewed on one afternoon a week in summer. From the sweeping parkland, distant views of the cathedral remind one of another age when – who knows – perhaps Francis Bacon did write some of Shakespeare's plays. A memorial to him can be found in St Michael's Church, directly opposite Verulamium Museum.

LEFT:
A bronze Venus found near the theatre.

RIGHT:
The Roman theatre on the Gorhambury estate.

INSET RIGHT:
A monument to Sir Francis Bacon in St Michael's Church, St Albans.

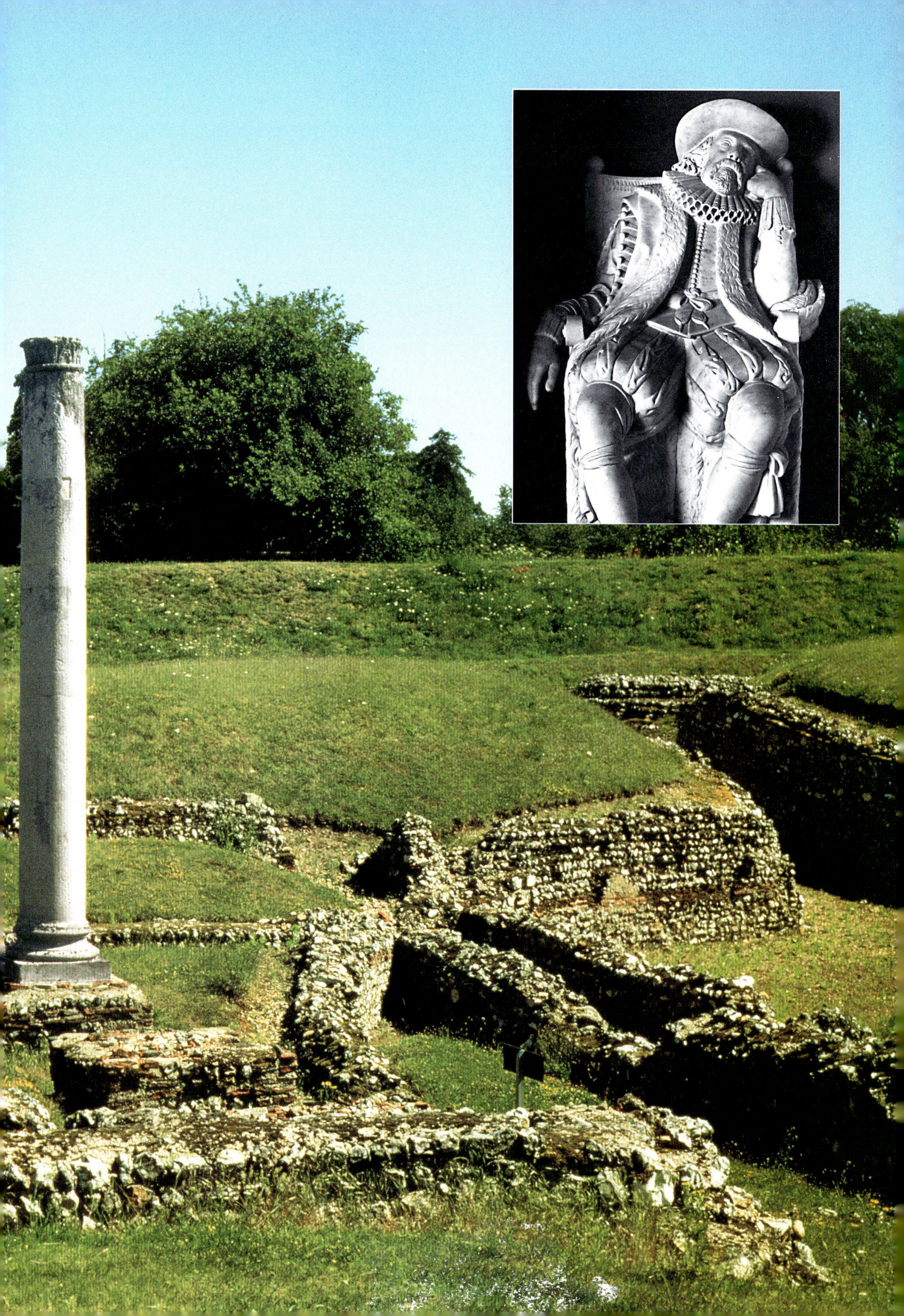

THE VILLAGES AROUND

The villages around St Albans each have their own special charm. St Michael's village, which lies above a section of the Roman city of Verulamium, is strictly part of St Albans. The mill located there retains the name of Kingsbury, after the later Saxon settlement in this vicinity. A highly popular restaurant in the mill buildings offers waffles and other homemade fare to be enjoyed while watching the millwheel turn. An example of the unique Hertfordshire puddingstone alongside the mill marks where the Mayor sets off each Rogation Sunday to 'beat the bounds' of the ancient borough.

This is just one of a series of mills along the Ver, some dating from medieval times. Recently restored and in working order is the delightful 18th-century Redbournbury mill, 2 miles (4km) from St Michael's along the Redbourn Road. The premises are available for private functions and delicious afternoon teas are served there on Sundays from April to October.

Picturesque Wheathampstead lies on the River Lea close to the Devil's Dyke. This defensive earthwork was built by Belgic tribes in the 1st century BC. John Bunyan is said to have lodged in a cottage at nearby Coleman Green on one of his missionary journeys from Bedford. A delightful pub opposite provides good food and rest for all the family.

Just off the B653 from Wheathampstead, a narrow country lane opens out into Ayot St Lawrence, the place forever associated with world-famous novelist and playwright George Bernard Shaw. After marrying in London, Shaw made his permanent home in the hamlet in 1906. He renamed the former vicarage 'Shaw's Corner' and lived there until his death in 1950. Shaw wrote prolifically in the revolving writing hut in his garden, besides entertaining the famous and riding around the country lanes on his bicycle.

Visit Ayot in July and see the house, full of Shaw's possessions, and the gardens at their best. Follow that with a cream tea at the ancient Brocket Arms nearby, or return in the evening to picnic and see one of Shaw's plays performed on the terrace. Or visit in May for the spectacular displays of bluebells in the woods around the Ayots.

ABOVE:
The study of George Bernard Shaw at his Ayot St Lawrence home.

RIGHT:
Kingsbury Mill at St Michael's village.

BELOW:
Redbournbury Mill.

*LEFT:
A summer scene by the River Lea at Wheathampstead.*

HATFIELD HOUSE

Just 5 miles (8km) along the old turnpike from St Albans up the Great North Road – or nowadays, less glamorously, along the A414 over the A1(M) – lies Hatfield House. It is the site of the royal palace where Elizabeth I spent much of her childhood, but the magnificent present house was built in 1611 by Robert Cecil, 1st Earl of Salisbury, Chief Minister to King James I. Hatfield remains in the Cecil family and is today the home of the current Marquess of Salisbury.

The state rooms of Hatfield are rich in world-famous paintings, exquisite furniture, fine tapestries and historic armour. Superb examples of Jacobean craftsmanship can be seen throughout the house, such as the grand staircase containing a wealth of lively detail carved in wood, and the rare stained glass window which is situated in the private chapel.

The park has several miles of marked trails, with picnic areas, gift shops and a restaurant; a full and varied programme of events takes place here from March to September. The original 17th-century gardens were laid out for the 1st Earl by the famous John Tradescant the Elder who introduced trees, bulbs and plants not previously grown in England. The present Marchioness has recreated the grounds in a style that reflects their Jacobean history, maintaining them organically. The west gardens, including the herb and knot gardens and a wilderness area, are open to the public at the same times as the house. Fridays are designated 'connoisseur days' when the house is reserved for the enjoyment of prebooked groups, but casual visitors can stroll in all 42 acres (17ha) of the park and formal gardens.

St Albans

ABOVE:
The grand staircase.

ABOVE LEFT:
The imposing front of Hatfield House.

LEFT:
The maze is situated in one of several beautiful gardens.

THE GARDENS OF THE ROSE

Garden lovers everywhere will know that perhaps the most stunning spectacle of roses in Britain can be found on the southern edge of St Albans, only a short distance from the M1 and M25. Here at Chiswell Green are the trial and display gardens of the Royal National Rose Society. With over 30,000 roses on show, set against a rich variety of companion plants, the gardens offer a captivating array of colour between April and September.

The original house provides a central focus for the garden, supporting climbers such as Summer Wine and the vigorous Kiftsgate. The south-facing terrace is an excellent starting point for a tour, with its vistas over the lawns and colourful borders. Not to be overlooked are the smaller gardens, including the recently established iris garden, from which visitors can draw inspiration for their own humbler plots.

Stroll through the Queen Mother Garden, with its fine collection of old-fashioned garden varieties including Bourbon and Damask roses, and the Peace Rose Garden, which demonstrates the important role this variety has played in the development of modern roses.

During the summer months, the 21-acre (8ha) grounds also provide a beautiful setting for wedding receptions, as well as for a number of other activities including gardening shows, flower shows, lunches and evening receptions, these taking place inside an elegant marquee. Also popular on summer evenings, when the fragrances can be even more alluring, are the open-air Shakespeare productions and concerts, including a wonderful 'Last Night at the Proms' in August.

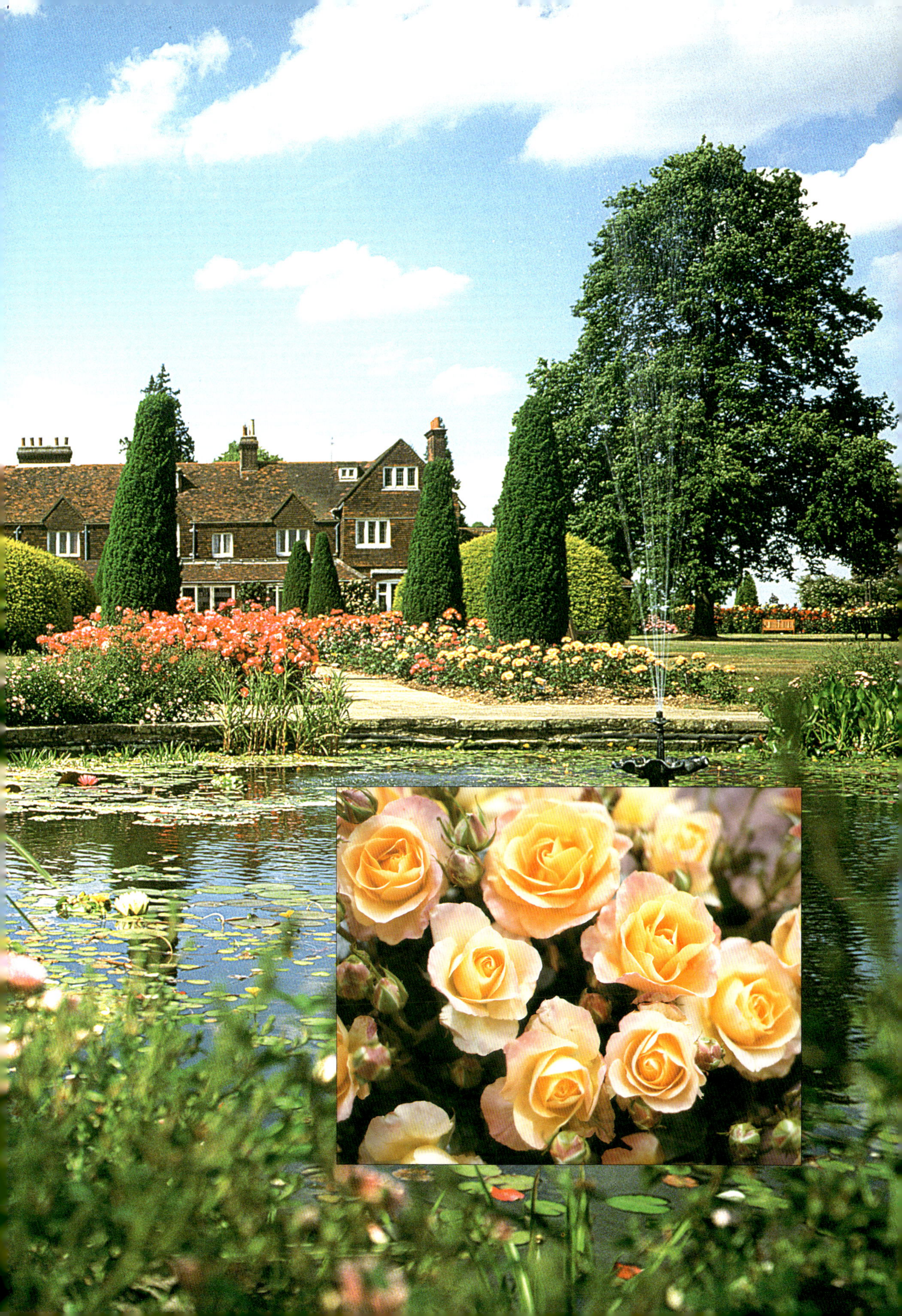

ST ALBANS

MUSEUMS

BOWMANS OPEN FARM

A day out for all the family, Bowmans is guaranteed to entrance the visitor, with its farm trail, pets' corner and falconry displays. Day tickets are available for fishing in the lakes and the 'touching barn' provides entertainment in all weathers. Who can resist the opportunity to cuddle a baby rabbit?

ST ALBANS ORGAN MUSEUM

Mortier, Decap and Bursens, Wurlitzer and Rutt – all are inspirational names to lovers of organs and mechanical musical instruments. These, together with musical boxes from the collection of the late Charles Hart, can be admired and enjoyed each Sunday afternoon in over two hours of pure nostalgia, and are guaranteed also to delight even the youngest child with their mellifluous magic.

VERULAMIUM MUSEUM

The award-winning Verulamium Museum tells the story of everyday life in a major Roman city through displays, videos, hands-on discovery areas and interactive computers. It features magnificent mosaics and wall plasters, recreated rooms and thousands of smaller objects used by the past inhabitants. The museum has an excellent shop which sells a wide range of gifts inspired by the past.

ABOVE:
Bowmans Open Farm.

ABOVE:
A fine mechanical organ by Mortier from the St Albans Organ Museum.

ST ALBANS

THE MUSEUM OF ST ALBANS

In a truly fascinating way, the Museum of St Albans tells the story of the modern city which grew around a great medieval abbey, illustrated through lively displays. The famous Salaman collection of trade and craft tools is here, as well as a wildlife garden and nature trail. The permanent displays are enhanced by a changing programme of special exhibitions. Admission is free.

ABOVE AND LEFT:
Just two of the many exhibits in the Museum of St Albans.

MOSQUITO MUSEUM

Pioneer aircraft engineer Sir Geoffrey De Havilland developed the historic Tiger Moth and the Mosquito, the versatile plywood-built fighter so successful in World War II. His company went on to develop many famous planes at its Hatfield site, including the world's first jet airliner, the Comet. To meet the need for engineers, a technical college was established nearby. This grew into the Hatfield Polytechnic, and is now the University of Hertfordshire. The museum at Salisbury Hall commemorates many De Havilland aircraft and offers hands-on opportunities for enthusiasts.

ABOVE:
A De Havilland Mosquito from the Mosquito Museum at Salisbury Hall.

Acknowledgements

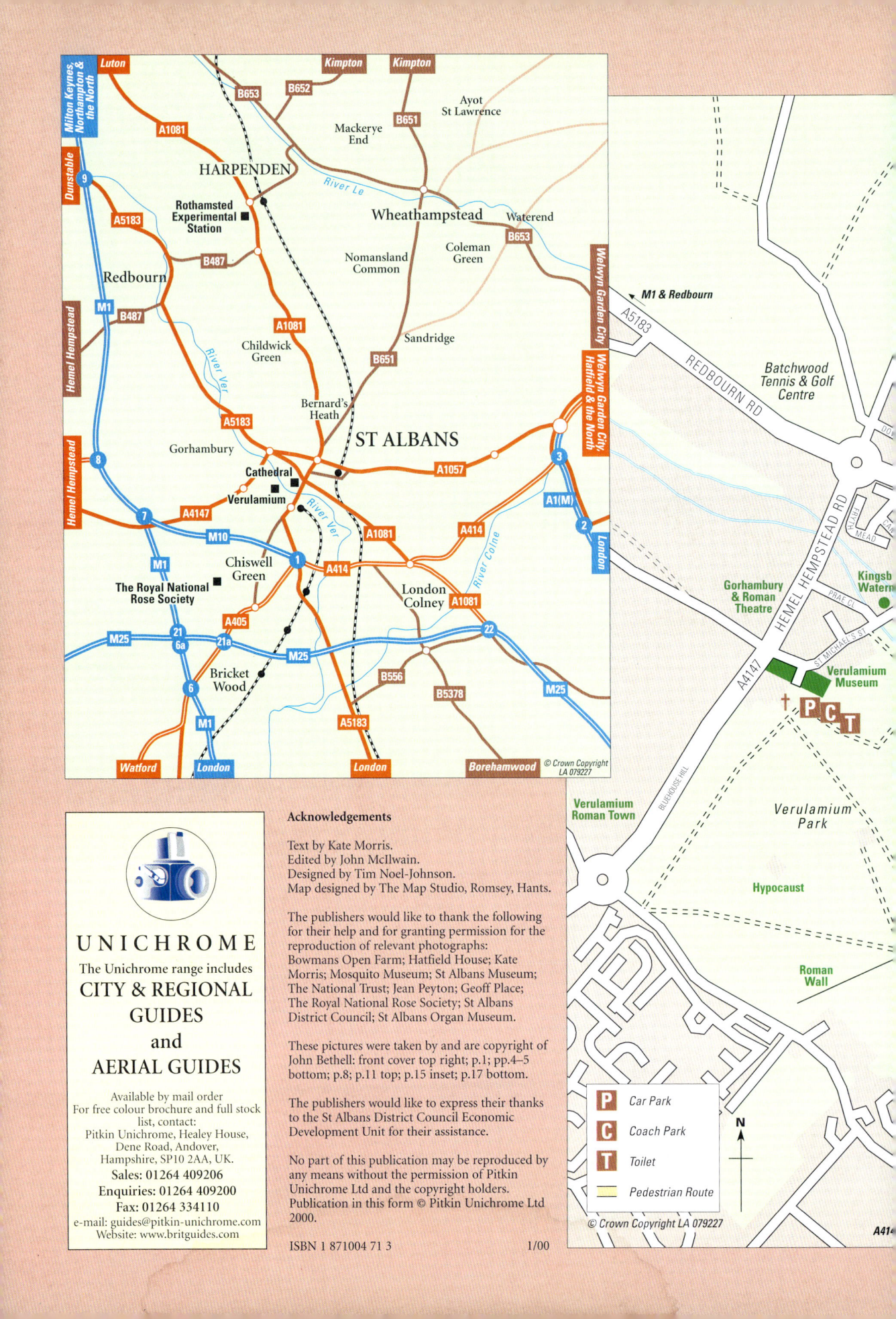

Text by Kate Morris.
Edited by John McIlwain.
Designed by Tim Noel-Johnson.
Map designed by The Map Studio, Romsey, Hants.

The publishers would like to thank the following for their help and for granting permission for the reproduction of relevant photographs: Bowmans Open Farm; Hatfield House; Kate Morris; Mosquito Museum; St Albans Museum; The National Trust; Jean Peyton; Geoff Place; The Royal National Rose Society; St Albans District Council; St Albans Organ Museum.

These pictures were taken by and are copyright of John Bethell: front cover top right; p.1; pp.4–5 bottom; p.8; p.11 top; p.15 inset; p.17 bottom.

The publishers would like to express their thanks to the St Albans District Council Economic Development Unit for their assistance.

No part of this publication may be reproduced by any means without the permission of Pitkin Unichrome Ltd and the copyright holders. Publication in this form © Pitkin Unichrome Ltd 2000.

ISBN 1 871004 71 3 1/00

UNICHROME

The Unichrome range includes
CITY & REGIONAL GUIDES
and
AERIAL GUIDES

Available by mail order
For free colour brochure and full stock list, contact:
Pitkin Unichrome, Healey House, Dene Road, Andover, Hampshire, SP10 2AA, UK.
Sales: 01264 409206
Enquiries: 01264 409200
Fax: 01264 334110
e-mail: guides@pitkin-unichrome.com
Website: www.britguides.com

Legend:
- P Car Park
- C Coach Park
- T Toilet
- Pedestrian Route

© Crown Copyright LA 079227